ONE LAST WALTZ

RENARD PRESS — PLAYSCRIPT VI

ONE LAST WALTZ:
FIRST PRODUCED BY BLACK COFFEE THEATRE FOR A UK TOUR IN 2015,
DIRECTED BY LUKE ADAMSON AND MARIA CROCKER.
MANDY PLAYED BY SUSAN MITCHELL,
ALICE PLAYED BY ANNIE SAWLE AND
GEORGETTE PLAYED BY ANDRINA CARROLL.

SECOND PRODUCTION AT
THE GREENWICH THEATRE IN 2018,
DIRECTED BY LUKE ADAMSON.
MANDY PLAYED BY JULIE BINYSH,
ALICE PLAYED BY AMANDA REED AND
GEORGETTE PLAYED BY JULIA FAULKNER.

ONE LAST WALTZ

LUKE ADAMSON

RENARD PRESS

RENARD PRESS LTD

124 City Road
London EC1V 2NX
United Kingdom
info@renardpress.com
020 8050 2928

www.renardpress.com

One Last Waltz first published by Renard Press Ltd in 2023

Text © Luke Adamson, 2023
Cover design by Will Dady

Printed in the United Kingdom by Severn

ISBN: 978-1-80447-027-5

9 8 7 6 5 4 3 2 1

CONTENTS

ONE LAST WALTZ

THIS PLAY IS DEDICATED TO THE MEMORY OF
ERNEST AND FRANCES WOOD.

NOTES

The play was written to be performed straight through with no interval, but one may be inserted if the director wishes.

The play is split into three parts, with each part focusing on the story of one character slightly more than the others, which mirrors the 3/4 time signature of a waltz. The choice of incidental music throughout is left to the director/sound designer, but it should all be in a 3/4 time signature. The original production used songs by Norah Jones, Damien Rice and Engelbert Humperdinck, as well as 'Are You Lonesome Tonight' by Elvis Presley before Part II, Scene 2.

The set can be designed as the designer and director want; in the original production it was constructed entirely out of cardboard boxes, and other bits of furniture, such as the reception desk, were built out of the boxes, with small costume changes happening onstage, with the costumes coming out of the boxes.

CHARACTERS

MANDY (50s): A single mother and doting daughter; looks in need of a rest.

ALICE (70s): Mandy's mother; witty and caring but stubborn; starting to have problems with her memory.

GEORGETTE (50s): An eccentric hotelier and a bit of a busybody.

PART ONE

MANDY

SCENE I

A room filled with boxes and moving cases that have never been unpacked. A waltz plays in the background. ALICE *enters. She moves to the nearest box and opens it, pulling out various items. Not finding what she was looking for, she moves on to the next box, pulling out more heirlooms and memories. Still not finding what she is looking for, she moves over to another box and pulls out more junk, followed by an old pair of dance shoes. She blows the dust off the shoes and looks at them more closely. Smiling, she takes her slippers off and pulls the dance shoes on, and begins to waltz in time with the music — gently at first, but eventually getting into it, until she is waltzing with flare and elegance. After a time she begins to tire, and, wheezing, she sits herself down and makes to take the shoes off. As she's doing so* MANDY *enters.*

MANDY: Mum?

ALICE: I'm here. Just having a sit down.

MANDY: Did you find them?

ALICE: Did I what?

MANDY: Did you find them?

ALICE (*thinks; then, after a pause*): I found the shoes.

MANDY: What?

ALICE: I found the shoes.

MANDY: What shoes?

ALICE (*pointing*): The shoes. The dance shoes. (*Pause.*) They were in that box.

MANDY: Mum…

ALICE: Yes?

MANDY: What did you come in here for?

ALICE (*pause*): Erm… I came… for the shoes?

MANDY: No, not for the shoes.

ALICE: No, not the shoes. The erm… The… I came in here to look for the… erm…

MANDY: The photographs.

ALICE: Yes.

MANDY: Remember?

ALICE: Yes. Yes, the photographs.

MANDY: Have you found them?

ALICE: I don't think so.

MANDY: You don't think so?

ALICE: No.

MANDY: Well, either you have or you haven't.

ALICE: I haven't.

MANDY: OK – where have you looked?

ALICE: In those boxes.

MANDY: Right. Well, you look in those ones, and I'll look in these, OK?

ALICE: Yes.

MANDY: And we're looking for…?

ALICE: Photographs.

MANDY: Photographs. Good.

(*They set about looking in boxes, pulling out old heirlooms. It is clear the boxes have sat unpacked for some time.*)

ALICE (*after a pause*): What photographs?

MANDY: The photo album with the old holiday pictures. Remember?

ALICE: Oh yes.

MANDY: Why haven't you unpacked these before?

ALICE: I never felt the need.

MANDY: You've been here years!

ALICE: Yes, but it's things I don't want on display.

MANDY: Well, you could unpack them at least?

ALICE: There's no point. You'll only have to repack them when I die.

MANDY: Oh, stop being so maudlin!

ALICE: Well, it's true. Everybody I know is dying. Gracie Foster died last week. And she's younger than me.

MANDY: She had a terminal illness.

ALICE: How do you know I haven't got one?

MANDY: Stop it, Mum.

ALICE: Well, it's true! I'm old. That's as good as any illness.

MANDY: Let's find these photos.

(There is silence as they look.)

ALICE: I could drop down tomorrow. Keel over in Morrison's.

MANDY: You won't keel over in Morrison's.

ALICE: How do you know?

MANDY: Tomorrow's Tuesday. We go shopping on Thursday.

ALICE: Is it? I thought today was Wednesday.

MANDY: No, it's Monday, Mum.

ALICE: Oh. But I put the bins out.

MANDY: I know – I brought them in again.

ALICE: Oh.

(They continue looking. MANDY *finds an old black-and-white picture in a frame.)*

MANDY: Oh, Mum – look at this! It's you and Dad.

ALICE: Let's see!

MANDY: When was this?

ALICE: Well, that's the tower in the background…

MANDY: Eiffel?

ALICE: Blackpool. We first went on holiday there in 1958.

MANDY: You should take this downstairs and put it on the mantelpiece.

ALICE: Ooh, no.

MANDY: Why not? It's a lovely picture of you and Dad.

ALICE: Not with that jumper.

MANDY: What?

ALICE: That jumper. It's a monstrosity.

MANDY: What's wrong with the jumper?

ALICE: I've always hated it. His aunty knitted it for him, so he used to insist on wearing it. No. I don't want that on display for all to see.

MANDY: Are you joking?

ALICE: No.

MANDY: The best photo of you and Dad that I've ever seen, and you won't put it up because of a jumper?

ALICE: Blue and green should never be seen.

MANDY: Blue and green? Where've you heard that?

ALICE: That's fashion law, that is.

MANDY: Oh, well if it rhymes…!

ALICE: I'm sure there's a better picture of us somewhere.

MANDY: Yeah, probably.

ALICE: I've got a whole album somewhere with loads of holiday pictures in. It's brown, I think. Or red.

MANDY: Photo album…

ALICE: Yeah. Full of pictures from holidays. It's in this box, I think.

(*She moves to an unopened box, opens it, rummages around and pulls out the album.*)

Here it is!

MANDY: Yeah. How did you…?

ALICE: Well, this is where I keep the photo albums.

MANDY: Right.

ALICE (*opening it and reading what is written inside the cover*): Scarborough 1957, Blackpool 1958, Whitby 1961.

MANDY: You got around.

ALICE: That's where you went in those days – the seaside. They used to organise bus trips.

MANDY: Which was your favourite?

ALICE: My favourite? My favourite what?

MANDY: Holiday.

ALICE: Out of these?

MANDY: Yes.

ALICE: Oh, Blackpool. Definitely.

MANDY: Really?

ALICE: Oh yeah. Scarborough was nice, and Whitby had the abbey – but Blackpool had the entertainment!

MANDY: The entertainment?

ALICE: Yes. Well, of course the others had entertainment too, but not like Blackpool. The 'luminations, the tower – there was all sorts!

MANDY: I'll bet there was!

ALICE: We saw Ken Dodd in Blackpool. Top of the bill!

MANDY: Ken Dodd!

ALICE: Oh, Mandy, he was brilliant. We went in at seven, and didn't come out until after midnight, still laughing!

MANDY: Oh, rubbish!

ALICE: It's not rubbish! The people sat next to us watched for about an hour then left. We couldn't believe it! But then they came back some time after ten, sat back down and watched another two hours!

MANDY: Two hours?

ALICE: They'd been and had a meal!

MANDY: In the middle of the show?

ALICE: In the middle of the show.

MANDY: Sounds like you had a good time.

ALICE: We did, we did. One night we went to this dinner-dance thing. We were put on this table, me and your dad, with all these other people we didn't know.

MANDY: Right.

ALICE: And we were sitting there, being all English – you know, not talking to each other, avoiding eye contact. And then all of a sudden this fat man came over with his wife, thrust his hand at your dad and exclaimed, 'Hi, I'm Stan. I'm from New York,' and he went round the whole table and introduced himself to everybody.

MANDY: Did he?

ALICE: And that broke the ice, you see, got us all talking.

MANDY: Yeah.

ALICE: Because we'd all been sitting in silence up until that point.

MANDY: Yeah, you said.

ALICE: And we had a great night! The dinner was lovely. We had a great chat to Stan and his wife – Cherie, I think it was, or Cheryl. We got talking to a couple from Welwyn Garden City that were sat on the other side of us. And then we all got up dancing.

MANDY: All of you?

ALICE: All of us. Well, Stan only lasted a couple of dances, but the rest of us were going all night. We did all sorts. Foxtrot. Jive – did you ever see your dad attempt to jive?

MANDY: I don't think so.

ALICE: Good. If I'd exposed you to that they'd have locked me up years ago!

MANDY: Bad, was he?

ALICE: The man couldn't jive to save his life! But he could waltz – my God, could he waltz! When that music came on he transformed. It's like he was a different man. He could move me round that floor like I was a feather. I've always enjoyed waltzing. Of course, I haven't done it properly recently. (*Slight pause.*) It'd be strange doing it again now without your dad.

MANDY: Would it?

ALICE: Sorry?

MANDY: Would it be strange doing it without him?

ALICE: I couldn't waltz with another man.

MANDY: What about me?

ALICE: You can waltz with whoever you like.

MANDY: No – I meant, could you waltz with me?

ALICE: But you're not a man.

MANDY: Does that matter?

ALICE: You wouldn't want to dance with me, would you?

MANDY: Why not? It could be fun.

ALICE: There's nowhere round here that does dances like that any more.

MANDY: Then let's go to Blackpool!

ALICE: Go to...?

MANDY: Blackpool. Yeah.

ALICE: No. I couldn't.

MANDY: Why not? We could go for a weekend, just you and me.

ALICE: No. No, I don't think so. Not at my age.

MANDY: It'd be nice – a bit of a holiday.

ALICE: No. I've had my Blackpool holiday. I've got my photographs and my memories, and that's all I need.

MANDY: Oh, come on, Mum. How long is it since you've had a holiday?

ALICE: No, Mandy. Not for me.

MANDY: A weekend in Blackpool. It'd be nice!

ALICE: It wouldn't be the same.

(ALICE *leaves, taking the dance shoes.* MANDY *sighs, picks up the photo album and looks through some of the pictures. She sees a picture of her dad and speaks aloud to him.*)

MANDY: Why'd you have to bugger off, eh? I wish you were here, Dad. It's getting tougher... Oh, she was right about that jumper... Blue and green, and with brown trousers...!

(*A waltz plays in the background as the scene changes then fades out.* MANDY *flicks through the album again. Suddenly a piece of paper flutters down from the album. She picks it up and reads it, then puts the album away, leaving the piece of paper on top of it.*)

SCENE 2

The following day. MANDY *stands, talking on the phone.*

MANDY: I know, love. Yes. Well, I'm at your grandma's again… What time?… Well, can you not get a lift home with Rachel's mum? I wish your dad wouldn't keep doing this… You think…? Have you met her? Is she prettier than me? (*Pause.*) Good answer! OK, I'll see if I can make it. Thanks, love. Bye. Bye.

ALICE (*entering*): Mandy? Who are you talking to?

MANDY: I was just on the phone to Emma.

ALICE: Is she all right?

MANDY: Her dad hasn't turned up to pick her up again. I'm going to have to go and get her.

ALICE: He was always a wrong 'un.

MANDY: I know. You told me often enough.

ALICE: You wouldn't listen! You've always been stubborn.

MANDY: Thanks, Mum!

ALICE: Still – he's that other hussy's problem now.

MANDY: Except when he's letting his daughters down…

ALICE: You're all better off without him.

MANDY: That's what I keep telling myself.

ALICE: Forget about him – if he doesn't want to be in their lives that's his problem.

MANDY: But he does! Well, he says he does.

ALICE: They'll say anything to stay in the good books.

MANDY: I suppose. He does love them.

ALICE: Of course he does, but he loves himself more.

MANDY: Did you want something?

ALICE: Can I talk to you about breakfast?

MANDY: Breakfast?

ALICE: Yeah, breakfast. I don't think I had any.

MANDY: Course you did.

ALICE: Did I?

MANDY: Yes. I was here.

ALICE: Oh. What did I have?

MANDY: What do you usually have?

ALICE: Well, I normally have a bowl of muesli and a glass of grapefruit juice.

MANDY: So what do you think you had this morning?

ALICE: I don't know.

MANDY: Mum, you had that. You had what you normally had.

ALICE: Did I?

MANDY: Yes.

ALICE: I don't remember.

MANDY: Course you don't.

ALICE: I had a lovely pasty the other day. Cornish.

MANDY: Did you?

ALICE: Yes. Best pasty I've ever had.

MANDY: Where did you get it from?

ALICE: I er... erm. (*Thinks.*) You brought it!

MANDY: Yeah. Mum, that was earlier this afternoon.

ALICE: No... No, it was... (*She checks her watch.*) Was it?

MANDY: Yeah.

ALICE: I thought...

MANDY: I know.

(ALICE *sees the piece of paper lying on top of the photo album.*)

ALICE: What's this?

MANDY: It fell out of the photo album.

ALICE (*reading*): The Crown Hotel... this is from Blackpool.

MANDY: Is it?

ALICE: It's where we stayed – me and your dad.

MANDY: You remember that?

ALICE: Oh yes. It was a lovely little place. Run by a family. More of a B&B than a hotel, really. Not quite on the front, but our room had a sea view.

MANDY: Sounds lovely.

ALICE: It was. We got to know all the other guests. All the staff.

MANDY: You don't get that these days.

ALICE: They used to leave little notes for you in the room when they'd tidied it. 'Hope you enjoyed the beach!' or 'How was Mr Dodd?' Made you feel really special.

MANDY: That's nice.

ALICE: It was.

MANDY: Well, my offer still stands. We could go if you fancied it.

ALICE: I don't know...

MANDY: We could go to the same hotel – see if it's how you remember it.

ALICE: I suppose.

MANDY: Go and see a show.

ALICE: Go dancing…

MANDY: Yeah. If you wanted.

(ALICE *stares at the piece of paper in her hand.*)

Look, Mum, I'm going to have to go – Emma's waiting
– but if you need anything, just give me a ring.

ALICE: OK.

MANDY: If I'm not at home try me on my mobile.

ALICE: All right, yes.

MANDY: Have you got your mobile?

ALICE: Yes, yes, I've got it here.

MANDY: And you remember how to use it?

ALICE: Mandy, I'm old, I'm not an idiot.

MANDY: Are you sure?

ALICE: Yes. It's easy – I put your number in, press a few
buttons and then give up and use the house phone.

MANDY: Very funny.

ALICE: Go on – I'll be fine.

MANDY: You sure?

ALICE: Emma's waiting.

MANDY: All right, OK. I'll see you tomorrow.

ALICE: OK, love.

MANDY: If you need anything, ring me.

ALICE: Go on. Give Emma my love!

MANDY: Yes. OK. I will. See you.

(MANDY *leaves* ALICE, *who stays, looking at the room. She sees the
photograph album, picks it up and starts to look through it. A waltz
starts to play in the background again as the scene changes then fades*

out. She smiles and looks away, then her eyes light on the shoes, and she reaches into her pocket and takes out her mobile phone. She looks at the piece of paper, dials the number and listens.)

ALICE: Out of service.

SCENE 3

ALICE *and* MANDY *enter.* MANDY *is carrying numerous packets of pills.*

MANDY: So this one's for your blood pressure, this one's for your heart and this one's for your poo—

ALICE: Oh, Mandy!

MANDY: What?

ALICE: There's no need to be so coarse!

MANDY: Well, what do you want me to say? 'This one's because you can't shit!'

ALICE: Amanda! Say 'stools'. The doctor says 'stools'.

MANDY: All right, fine. This one's for your blood pressure, this one's for your heart and this one's for your *stools*.

ALICE: See – that's better.

MANDY: Sounds ridiculous.

ALICE: It doesn't!

MANDY: Sounds like I'm talking about furniture.

ALICE: I'll never remember all that.

MANDY: Well, you'll have to.

ALICE: Oh, what's the point? Let's be honest, I'll probably be dead by Christmas, whether I take them or not.

MANDY: Oh, stop it, Mum!

ALICE: I'm only being realistic.

MANDY: I'll leave them in the kitchen, and I'll write down which ones you have to take and when. OK?

ALICE: If you must.

MANDY: I must.

(MANDY *makes to leave.*)

ALICE: Mandy?

MANDY: Yeah?

ALICE: Were you really serious − about going to Blackpool?

MANDY: Yeah. Let's do it − it'll be fun. Have a paddle, see the illuminations…

ALICE: Have a dance in the ballroom.

MANDY: And a cream tea. Sod it. Let's go crazy!

ALICE: I tried to ring them yesterday, but the number on that card is out of service.

MANDY: It would be. It's nearly sixty years old.

ALICE: Well, I didn't know.

MANDY: I had a look online and I found the new number. Here.

(MANDY *passes* ALICE *a post-it note with a phone number on.*)

ALICE: Hm.

MANDY: So are you in?

ALICE: Oh, I don't know. I can't just go gallivanting about at my age. These things need planning. I'll probably need injections or something.

MANDY: It's Blackpool, Mum, not Belize!

ALICE: Yes, well.

MANDY: So are we going?

ALICE: Weren't you going to get me something?

MANDY: I was going to write your prescriptions down so you knew—

ALICE: Well, get on with it, then! We haven't got for ever.

(ALICE *takes out the photo album and starts flicking through.*)

MANDY: Right, OK, yes. (*Leaving, with the pill boxes:*) Remember: Heart, blood pressure, poo.

ALICE: Stools! Oh, she's coarse. She gets that from you, George. She gets her brains from me, luckily, and her dress sense, but she got your nose, poor girl. (*She continues to look through the pictures.*) They say only the good die young, so why did you go before me? Look at you, distracting me again. It was bad enough you distracting me when you were alive – never mind from beyond the grave! Stop distracting me, you supernatural bastard. Pardon my French. Oh, that pigging jumper. Heavens to Murgatroyd! I can't look at it. It's offensive. Oh, what was I doing? Mandy? Mandy!

MANDY: What? What is it?

ALICE: What was I doing?

MANDY: What?

ALICE: What was I supposed to be doing? I got distracted by your dad.

MANDY: You got distracted by Dad?

ALICE: Yeah, pictures of your dad.

MANDY: Oh, thank God for that. I thought you thought you'd been talking to the dead.

ALICE: Don't be stupid! You don't believe in all that claptrap, do you?

MANDY: No! It's just when you said you'd been... Anyway, I've written all the pills on a note and left it on the side next to the kettle.

ALICE: Kettle, yes. What've you written down?

MANDY: Your prescriptions.

ALICE: Oh yes. Oh, thanks for reminding me – I've got a doctor's appointment this afternoon! Dr Edwards. You couldn't give me a lift, could you? I was late last time.

MANDY: A lift?

ALICE: To the doctor's, yeah.

MANDY: Mum, we've just got back from the doctor's.

ALICE: Don't be silly. It's this afternoon.

MANDY: Mum, we've just got back – that's why I was in the kitchen writing down which pill you have to take when and what it's for. I was there with you.

ALICE: Mandy, what on earth are you talking about? I've got an appointment with Dr... erm. Oh, Dr... I just had it. That woman doctor. The one I saw about my cough.

MANDY: Dr Edwards. Mum, we were just there!

ALICE: Were we? Oh.

MANDY: Mum. I think we should see someone about your memory. You've been forgetting quite a lot recently.

ALICE: See somebody? Oh, Mandy, stop overreacting.

MANDY: Mum, I'm being serious, it's worrying me.

ALICE: It's only little things! We all forget little things from time to time.

MANDY: It's not just from time to time, though, is it? It's every day, and it's not just small things.

ALICE: Amanda, listen to me. There's nothing wrong with me. If there were I'd be the first to worry.

MANDY: But you don't realise when—

ALICE: We're not having this conversation.

MANDY: Fine.

ALICE: And I think we should go.

MANDY: Sorry?

ALICE: Blackpool. Let's go.

MANDY: Are you sure?

ALICE: Yes. I said so, didn't I? I might not get another chance for a holiday.

MANDY: Right. Well…

ALICE: We can go next week, like you said.

MANDY: Why the sudden change of heart?

ALICE: What – a person can't change their mind?

MANDY: No, it's just—

ALICE: Can't a crazy person have a holiday?

MANDY: I never said you were crazy!

ALICE: You never said it, no…

MANDY: I never thought it either! I'm just worried about your memory, that's all.

ALICE: Well, then, let's go to Blackpool and make some new memories before I'm too batty to remember anything.

MANDY: You really want to?

ALICE: Oh, for Christ's sake. Never mind.

MANDY: No. Let's do it. Let's go.

ALICE: No, don't worry!

MANDY: Yes. We're going.

ALICE: Good. It'll be nice to go back. See if things have changed. Have another dance in the ballroom.

MANDY: Even without Dad?

ALICE: Even without Dad. To dance with you will be a pleasure.

(*Pause.* MANDY *smiles.*)

If you can stop making out I'm a lunatic, Now, go and make me a cup of tea, I'll give that hotel a ring.

MANDY: Are you sure? I can ring them.

ALICE: I'm not totally useless. Go on.

MANDY: Fine. OK.

(MANDY *leaves.* ALICE *takes out her mobile phone and dials the number on the post-it.*)

ALICE: Hello. Yes. Do you have any rooms available next week? Yes. For two people. Double? Yes. What's the difference? Oh, twin. Twin! Absolutely. Miss Alice Cartwright, 69 Marchmont Avenue…

(*The lights fade.*)

PART TWO

GEORGETTE

SCENE I

The Crown Hotel, Blackpool. GEORGETTE *is busying herself behind the reception counter.* MANDY *enters, followed by* ALICE. *They have suitcases.*

ALICE: Are you sure?

MANDY: I'm sure!

ALICE: It doesn't look the same.

MANDY: It's over fifty years since you were last here, Mum – chances are it's changed a bit!

ALICE: No, it's not the same. It's a different place.

MANDY: Well, this is the one you've booked, all right?

ALICE: I don't understand why they'd feel the need to change it.

MANDY (*to* GEORGETTE): Hi there.

GEORGETTE: Hello! Welcome to the Crown Hotel. Do you have a reservation?

MANDY: Yes – it'll be under Simpson.

GEORGETTE: Certainly. I'll just check. (*She pulls out a large leather-bound tome.*)

ALICE: They used to have a coat rack by the door so you could hang your coat up when it had been raining.

GEORGETTE: Simpson, you say?

MANDY: Yes.

GEORGETTE: Checking in today?

MANDY: Yes...

ALICE: And a little telephone table with a phone, so you could make calls.

MANDY (to ALICE): They have those in the room these days. (*To* GEORGETTE:) Is there a problem?

ALICE: Do they? Oh! I wouldn't like that. People being able to contact you day and night.

GEORGETTE: I can't seem to find the booking. When was it made?

MANDY: Wednesday, I think.

ALICE: They used to give us a sherry before our evening meal – I don't suppose they'll do that any more!

GEORGETTE: And it was definitely under Simpson?

MANDY: I think so...

GEORGETTE: Well, it's not here.

MANDY: Are you sure? (*Tries to look at the book.*)

GEORGETTE: Step back please, madam. It's guest confidentiality, I'm afraid.

ALICE: And the manager would come round daily and check that everything was all right.

GEORGETTE: I can't be seen to allow you access to all of their personal details.

MANDY: All of their...?

GEORGETTE: Of course, then I start to wonder if you're actual guests at all, or if you're just trying to pry into the details of our esteemed visitors.

ALICE: Oh. No. It is the same. I remember that spider plant.

MANDY: Please. I've had a long drive, and I'd really like to put our bags in the room and have a cuppa. It must be there somewhere.

GEORGETTE: Under Simpson?

MANDY: Yes.

GEORGETTE: No. I've got nothing. Could it be Sampson?

MANDY: Have you got a booking under Sampson?

GEORGETTE: No, I just thought you might be getting the name wrong.

MANDY: Mum, you did make the booking, didn't you?

ALICE: Of course I did!

MANDY: What name is it under?

ALICE: Cartwright.

MANDY: Cartwright?

ALICE: Yes.

MANDY: Mum, you haven't used that name in nearly sixty years.

GEORGETTE: Ah, yes. There we are – Cartwright. Twin room, checking in today.

MANDY: Thank God for that! Are you busy, then?

GEORGETTE: Oh no, there's only you two here over the weekend.

MANDY: Only us two?

GEORGETTE: Yeah.

MANDY: We were the only booking?

GEORGETTE: Yes.

MANDY: And it still took you that long to find us in the book...

GEORGETTE: Well, it's security, isn't it. Can't be too careful. Anyone can come in off the street, saying they've booked a room. Pick a common surname like Simpson and chance their arm. Get a holiday at someone else's expense!

ALICE: I've stayed here before.

GEORGETTE: Ah, it's a joy to have you back!

ALICE: In 1958.

GEORGETTE: Oh, how lovely.

ALICE: I don't remember you, though.

GEORGETTE: From 1958! How old do you think I am?

MANDY: Could we just have the keys, please.

GEORGETTE: Key.

MANDY: Sorry?

GEORGETTE: There's one key.

MANDY: But there are two of us.

ALICE: I don't like that wallpaper.

GEORGETTE: One room, one key.

ALICE: Too many stripes.

MANDY: OK, one key. Do you have it?

ALICE: It's giving me a headache.

GEORGETTE: Of course I have it, it's an hotel!

ALICE: Hope it's not like that in the room!

GEORGETTE: It's in the back. I won't be a second. (*Leaves.*)

ALICE: Do you think it will be?

MANDY: What?

ALICE: Do you think it will be like that in the room?

MANDY: Be like what in the room?

ALICE: Stripy. The wallpaper.

MANDY: How would I know, Mum? How the hell would I know what the wallpaper is like in a room I've never been in?

ALICE: There's no need to shout.

GEORGETTE: Here we are. Room six. First floor. End of the corridor.

ALICE: Thank you.

(ALICE *takes the key and leaves.* MANDY *sighs. There is a pause. After a moment* GEORGETTE *reaches under the desk, takes out a bottle of scotch and thumps it down on the desk.*)

GEORGETTE: Large?
MANDY: I beg your pardon?
GEORGETTE: I've seen that look before. Large?
MANDY: I don't drink scotch.
GEORGETTE: Bourbon?
MANDY: Not really.
GEORGETTE: Gin? Vodka? Rum? I've got them all.
MANDY: No, thank you.
GEORGETTE: Well, all you have to do is ask.
MANDY: Thanks.
GEORGETTE: First one's on the house.
MANDY: Very kind.
GEORGETTE: Any time.

(MANDY *picks up her bag and heads for the door.*)

I went through the same thing with my mum.

(MANDY *stops.*)

MANDY: Went through what?
GEORGETTE: Alzheimer's.
MANDY: Oh. It's not Alzheimer's, she's just a bit forgetful sometimes.
GEORGETTE: That's what I thought at first.

MANDY: What makes you think it's Alzheimer's?

GEORGETTE: Booking the room in her maiden name…

MANDY: It's an easy mistake to make. It happens as you get older.

GEORGETTE: I don't want to push it, I just want you to know that I'm here if you need to… talk.

MANDY: Thanks…

GEORGETTE: Georgette.

MANDY: Georgette. That's a nice name. Unusual.

GEORGETTE: Is it?

MANDY: Do they call you George for short?

GEORGETTE: No.

MANDY: Oh.

GEORGETTE: That's a man's name.

MANDY: Yes, it was my dad's name.

(ALICE *enters.*)

ALICE: Mandy, do you have my knickers?

MANDY: What? Why would I have your knickers?

ALICE: They're not in my case.

MANDY: What do you mean, they're not in your case?

ALICE: They're not in my case, so I thought they might be in yours.

MANDY: Why would they be in my case?

ALICE: I don't know.

MANDY: Have you forgotten to pack them?

ALICE: Well… I don't know.

MANDY: What do you mean you don't know?

ALICE: Well, they're not in my case.

MANDY: So you've forgotten to pack them?

ALICE: I swear I put them in.
MANDY: Come on, let's have a look.
GEORGETTE: There's a Primark. Fifteen minutes' walk.
ALICE: I'm sure I put them in...

(*They leave.*)

SCENE 2

Later that evening. GEORGETTE *sits, enjoying a glass of wine after a long day.* MANDY *enters.*

MANDY: Good evening.

GEORGETTE: Oh, hi. Sorry. I was just having a bit of 'down time'.

MANDY: Oh, please don't mind me. I might join you.

GEORGETTE: Please do.

MANDY: Is the bar open?

GEORGETTE: The bar is always open!

MANDY: Excellent!

GEORGETTE: Metaphorically.

MANDY: Sorry?

GEORGETTE: Metaphorically. I mean, don't be ringing me at four in the morning asking for a nightcap.

MANDY: I wouldn't.

GEORGETTE: It's always open… within reason.

MANDY: Right. Is it open now?

GEORGETTE: Of course! What would you like?

MANDY: A glass of wine?

GEORGETTE: Red or white?

MANDY: Do you have rosé?

GEORGETTE (*looking at the bottles*): I could make some…?

MANDY: Red's fine!

GEORGETTE (*reading*): It says it goes well with red meats and cheeses.

MANDY: Perfect.

GEORGETTE: Have you had a nice first day?

MANDY: Eventually, thank you.

GEORGETTE: Did you find them?

MANDY: Find what?

GEORGETTE: Your mum's knickers – did you…?

MANDY: Oh. No. But we did find the Primark. Thanks for that.

GEORGETTE: No problem.

MANDY: And then we had a nice walk around the town.

GEORGETTE: Lovely.

MANDY: We went down to the seafront. Had some fish and chips.

GEORGETTE: I bet your mum liked that.

MANDY: I thought she would, but she just kept moaning about how much everything has changed.

GEORGETTE: Since 1958? I would think it probably has.

MANDY: She kept trying to find places she went to back then – we were walking around in circles for hours.

GEORGETTE: Yes. They'll do that.

MANDY: Yes. 'They'?

GEORGETTE: Old people.

MANDY: Right.

(*They drink.*)

GEORGETTE: So. Why Blackpool? If you don't mind me asking.

MANDY: No, course not. Mum came here in 1958, as she mentioned, and the highlight of her holiday was waltzing in the ballroom with my dad.

GEORGETTE: Oh, how romantic!

MANDY: Well, she said she fancied waltzing in that same ballroom one last time before she keels over.

GEORGETTE: So you thought better sooner than later?

MANDY: Sorry?

GEORGETTE: Sorry?

MANDY: What did you say?

GEORGETTE: Who suggested this week? Hardly peak of the season.

MANDY: Well, I've been given a bit of compassionate leave, so I was off work anyway. It seemed to make sense. Get away for a bit. Remember the good times.

GEORGETTE: Yes. And it's given me a bit of company.

MANDY: Yes.

(*They drink.*)

GEORGETTE: Tower Ballroom?

MANDY: Sorry?

GEORGETTE: The Tower Ballroom?

MANDY: Yeah. We're going over there tomorrow.

GEORGETTE: You won't be getting in there any time soon.

MANDY: What do you mean?

GEORGETTE: It's closed – for major refurbishment.

MANDY: The ballroom?

GEORGETTE: Yeah. It's been bought by some business mogul. They're turning it into a casino.

MANDY: You're joking?

GEORGETTE: No. It was struggling to get by. The days of people popping in for a cream tea and a bit of a dance are long gone. It was only being used for the odd dance competition and occasional bits of filming – other than that it was sitting there empty.

MANDY: It's completely closed?

GEORGETTE: Big wooden boards all round it say so!

MANDY: Oh no! Mum will be heartbroken.

GEORGETTE: I'm sure she'll get over it.

MANDY: Yes, maybe. I'll tell her tomorrow. See what she says.

GEORGETTE: OK.

MANDY: It's probably best coming from me.

GEORGETTE: Of course – I understand.

(*Pause. They drink.*)

MANDY: You said earlier that your mum suffered with—

GEORGETTE: Alzheimer's. Yes.

MANDY: How… How was it?

GEORGETTE: It was hard. I won't lie. It was tough at first, and just got tougher.

MANDY: Right.

GEORGETTE: Seeing someone that has always been in your life slowly disappear until eventually they don't even know who you are… It's hard.

MANDY: Yeah. It must have been. When did you start to realise things weren't quite right?

GEORGETTE: It was small things at first – confusing names, putting things in the wrong places, asking the same questions over and over again.

MANDY: Did you know what it was straight away?

GEORGETTE: No! We just thought she was getting a bit forgetful. It was a year or so before we got a definite diagnosis.

MANDY: So it was quite a slow decline, then?

GEORGETTE: It didn't seem it. But then it varied. Some days she wouldn't even know her own name, and the next she'd be as right as rain.

MANDY: Right.

GEORGETTE: And if anyone came round to observe her she'd up her game. She was proud, you see. Always put on a performance.

MANDY: How did you deal with it?

GEORGETTE: I, erm, found a way.

MANDY: Fancy sharing it?

GEORGETTE: Well, we found the best way was to be patient. Don't tell her off for making mistakes, encourage her not to make the same mistakes again. She will, but you have to persevere. Don't lose your temper – that's when you say and do things you regret.

MANDY: Who's 'we'?

GEORGETTE: Sorry?

MANDY: You said 'we'. Are you married?

GEORGETTE: Oh! No. My sister and I. No, I've never been married.

MANDY: Right. Still, it must have been quite nice to have someone else there?

GEORGETTE: It... was. Yes.

(*She drinks.*)

I'm empty. Do you want a top-up?

MANDY: If you don't mind?

GEORGETTE: Of course not. I'd only be sitting here drinking
on my own, anyway.

MANDY: Thank you. Do you often unwind with a glass of
wine?

GEORGETTE: Most nights these days. I find it helps me relax.
Forget about... things.

MANDY: De-stresses you?

GEORGETTE: Exactly.

(*They drink. There is a pause.*)

MANDY: Are there many other staff?

GEORGETTE: Staff? No, not these days. Charlie the
gardener comes round once a week. And Tom – a
local boy – helps out occasionally. Well... I say 'helps'.
He's about as useful as a peanut-butter teapot, but
it's nice to have the company. You know, I saw him
cycling here the other day, and when he was turning
into the end of the street, instead of putting his arm
out like this, like you're supposed to, he stuck his
arm behind him and 'flashed' his hand like a car
indicator. Idiot.

MANDY (*laughing*): Ah! Hardly the next Einstein.

GEORGETTE: Frankenstein, maybe – I'm not sure about
Einstein.

MANDY: Well, maybe I'll get to meet him at some point.
Right, I'd best be getting to bed. Thanks for the drink.

GEORGETTE: Oh, you're not going yet, are you? We should
    at least finish the bottle.
MANDY: I shouldn't really.
GEORGETTE: Come on! You're on holiday!
MANDY: Yeah, I suppose I am!

(*A waltz plays in the background as the lights fade and the scene changes
then fades out.*)

SCENE 3

The next morning. ALICE *has come down for her breakfast. She is carrying her dance shoes.*

ALICE: Hello? Hello!

GEORGETTE (*less than sprightly*): Morning. You're up early.

ALICE: Yes, well, you know what they say.

GEORGETTE: Do I?

ALICE: About the early bird.

GEORGETTE: What do they say?

ALICE: The early bird catches the worm.

GEORGETTE: Right. Who says that?

ALICE: I don't know – people. It's a saying.

GEORGETTE: Is it?

ALICE: Yes.

GEORGETTE: It's a new one on me.

ALICE: I thought it was quite well known.

GEORGETTE: Apparently not. Do excuse me – I had quite a late night. I shared a couple of bottles of wine with Mandy.

ALICE: Oh, did you? That's why she's making noises like a harpooned walrus this morning. I see.

49

GEORGETTE: Yes, sorry about that. So, what would you like for your breakfast? (*Very slowly:*) We have the full English: sausage, bacon, egg, beans, hash browns, tomato and toast, and that comes with a glass of orange juice and a tea or a coffee; or we have the continental breakfast: a croissant or a pain o' chocolate, and that comes with an espresso and a cigarette. I am of course joking about the cigarette. What would you like?

ALICE: I'm sorry, I didn't catch all of that. Could you repeat it?

GEORGETTE: Of course, madam. We have the full English: sausage, bacon, egg, beans, hash browns, tomato and toast, and that comes with a glass of orange juice and a tea or a coffee; or we have the continental breakfast: a croissant or a pain o' chocolate, and that comes with an espresso, a cigarette and a string of onions. I am of course joking about those last two items.

ALICE: That all seems quite a lot.

GEORGETTE: We could do a variation on a theme for you? Sausage sandwich? Scrambled eggs on toast? Baked beans on a croissant?

ALICE: I normally have a bowl of muesli and a glass of grapefruit juice.

GEORGETTE: Right.

ALICE: Do you have anything like that?

GEORGETTE: Muesli and grapefruit juice?

ALICE: Yes.

GEORGETTE: No.

ALICE: Oh, but that's what I usually have.

GEORGETTE: I'm afraid with it being the off season we have less of a selection.

ALICE: Oh dear.

GEORGETTE: Maybe you'd like to try the continental?

ALICE: Yes, maybe. What's that?

GEORGETTE: A croissant or pain o' chocolate.

ALICE: Oh, I don't want chocolate for my breakfast. Who has chocolate for their breakfast?

GEORGETTE: The continentals, apparently.

ALICE: Oh no, that's not right.

GEORGETTE: A croissant, then?

ALICE: A croissant, yes. And a coffee.

GEORGETTE: Excellent. (*Shouting off:*) Tom, get a croissant out of the freezer and stick it in the microwave for me.

ALICE: It'll be like being in Paris!

GEORGETTE: It'll be just like that – but without the French people.

ALICE: Excellent. That's what's always put me off France, the French.

GEORGETTE: We had a French family stay here once. It was very confusing – they all had two names. Amelie-Renée, Jean-Claude, Marie-... Antoinette? Terribly confusing.

ALICE: And I suppose they'd insist on using both names?

GEORGETTE: Oh yes. Especially Jean-Claude. But that I can kind of understand that, because otherwise he's just Jean. That's not a great name for a man.

ALICE: Yes, but they pronounce it 'John', don't they?

GEORGETTE: Oh, do they?

ALICE: Yes, so it's like John Claude.

GEORGETTE: Oh, OK. I suppose that works in France, but in Blackpool we pronounce it 'Jean'. If he wanted to be called John he should have spelt it John.

ALICE: I suppose you're right.

GEORGETTE (*pointing at* ALICE*'s shoes*): Those are nice.

ALICE: Oh, thank you. They're my dance shoes.

GEORGETTE: How lovely.

ALICE: I've had them for years – I'm surprised they're still in one piece. I used to dance in them all the time. My George bought them for me. I'm going to have one last dance at the Tower Ballroom in them before they get shelved for ever.

GEORGETTE: Oh. Did Mandy not tell you?

ALICE: Tell me what? It was her idea, I think. We were looking for something – I can't remember what – and we came across these. I explained what they were, and she said we should come back to Blackpool for one last dance.

GEORGETTE: You'll have a job.

ALICE: That's what I said! I'm not sure my hips are quite up to it these days, but it'll be nice for the experience more than anything.

GEORGETTE: No, I mean—

ALICE: Of course, it'll be strange dancing there without George, but I know he'll be looking down smiling. I'm actually quite looking forward to it. Oh, sorry – look at me prattling on. What were you saying?

GEORGETTE: It's not really my place… I think you should speak to Mandy.

ALICE: Oh no, go on – don't worry.

GEORGETTE: Well, it's just that the Tower Ballroom has been… erm… closed.

ALICE: Closed?

GEORGETTE: Closed down, yes.

ALICE: When you say closed down…?

GEORGETTE: They've shut it off to the public – they're planning on turning it into a casino.

ALICE: A casino?

GEORGETTE: I'm afraid so.

ALICE: So we can't go dancing?

GEORGETTE (*visibly awkward*): Where's Tom with that croissant? (*Leaves.*)

ALICE (*looking at the shoes in her hands*): Well. It seems we can't go – sorry, shoes. We can't go. Sorry for getting your hopes up, but it's back to the cupboard. I'd got my hopes up too. Oh, I've been a fool. It's stupid to get excited about things at my age. I'll pop you away. (*She starts to leave, but then stops.*) But maybe we should go and see it anyway – just have a look. I'm sure I know the way. (*She clutches the shoes to her and walks out.*)

GEORGETTE (*off*): One croissant coming right up, but I'm afraid the coffee machine is on the blink – are you all right with Nescafé? Hello? Hello? (*Enters holding the croissant.*) Here's your breakfast! Oh.

(MANDY *enters, hungover, speaking on her mobile.*)

MANDY: No, love, she's all right. She's forgetting a few things. Well, she forgot to bring any knickers, for a start. Yeah. Then we went for a walk around the town, and she insisted on taking me to a certain café she'd been to before, but we'd been walking for fifteen minutes and then she turned and asked me where we were going. I said we were going to the café, and she asked me which one. I said, 'The one you wanted to take me to!', and she said, 'How would I know where the café is?' She keeps asking me what she's doing, as well. She'll be quite happily sitting there, reading or watching the TV, then she'll suddenly get up and say, 'What am I doing?' She woke up last night during the night and couldn't remember where she was. I don't know, Em. I want to take her to the doctor's – get her checked out. I know she's stubborn, but it's for her own good. They say the earlier they spot things the easier it is to treat. Well, I don't know. Alzheimer's. Well, it could be. We'll see when we get back. I'll have to try and convince her. OK, OK, love, say hello to your dad for me. Cheers, love. Bye.

GEORGETTE: Offspring?

MANDY: Daughter, Emma. Oh, perfect, I'm starving. (*Takes the croissant.*)

GEORGETTE: Is she all right?

MANDY: Oh, she's fine – just checking up on her grandma.

GEORGETTE: How are you feeling this morning?

MANDY: I've been better.

GEORGETTE: It's nice to let your hair down sometimes!

MANDY: Yeah. I think I needed a bit of time to unwind.

GEORGETTE: I'm just making some Nescafé – would you like one?

MANDY: Yes, please – black, two sugars.

GEORGETTE: Sure.

MANDY: Has my mum been down?

GEORGETTE: Yes, I was just talking to her.

MANDY: How was she?

GEORGETTE: Seemed fine. A little annoyed that we didn't have any muesli or grapefruit juice.

MANDY: Standard. Where is she now?

GEORGETTE: Did she not go back to the room?

MANDY: I didn't pass her on the way down, no.

GEORGETTE: Oh. Well, she was just here, then I went for the croissant, and then she wasn't here, and then you were here.

MANDY: She just left?

GEORGETTE: I assumed she'd gone back up to the room.

MANDY: Had she eaten her breakfast?

GEORGETTE: No – that croissant was for her.

MANDY: I don't know why she'd just leave... I'll try her mobile. (*Does.*)

GEORGETTE: I thought it was quite odd – one minute we were having a chat about France and dancing and things, and then she was off.

MANDY: She's not answering the phone. Probably can't hear it.

GEORGETTE: I have to admit, though, that I did say something I didn't mean to.

MANDY: What do you mean?

GEORGETTE: Well, I told her what I told you about the ballroom being closed.

MANDY: You told her?

GEORGETTE: Yes, sorry.

MANDY: How did she take it?

GEORGETTE: I don't know – I went to check on the croissant.

MANDY: Well, that'll be where she's gone. She will have gone to check what you said. She'll be looking for the tower.

GEORGETTE: Right.

MANDY: She can't be wandering around Blackpool on her own – she'll get lost! She hasn't got a clue where she's going.

GEORGETTE: I'm sure she'll be fine.

MANDY: Be fine! How can you think that? I'm going to have to go and find her. Did I not say that I wanted to tell her?

GEORGETTE: I didn't mean any harm – it just… came out.

MANDY: Oh, that's all right, then, if it just came out!

GEORGETTE: I didn't mean to – I wasn't thinking straight.

MANDY: I don't believe this! (*Storms out.*)

GEORGETTE: Mandy. Mandy! (*Exits, following.*)

PART THREE

ALICE

SCENE I

ALICE *walks along the blustery seafront, clutching her shoes to her chest. Her mobile rings in her pocket.*

ALICE: Blackpool, George. Do you remember? I'm in Blackpool. There's the sea, look, and the 'luminations. It's not quite how I remember it, though, George. You wouldn't like it. Things have changed so fast. The hotel's different. The town has changed. That used to be a café, didn't it? It's an amusement arcade now. What do I want with an amusement arcade? No, you wouldn't like it here these days, George. It's all different. All different. (*Pause.*) What was I doing? Oh, George, I've forgotten what I was doing. I'm a bit forgetful these days, you know. (*Seeing the shoes in her arms:*) Oh! I'm going for a dance – of course I am. I'm off for a dance at the ballroom. I'm going to waltz with Mandy. That'll be nice, won't it? It won't be the same as waltzing with you, but it'll be nice. One, two, three. One, two, three. One, two, three. Waltzing. Oh, look at that sea, George. It's quite fierce out there today. Remember when we used to paddle? You'd roll your trouser legs up and I'd laugh myself silly when one of them fell down and got wet. You had to walk all the way back to the hotel with a damp leg. All the way to the... Where is it? It's gone. George? George, the hotel's gone. The hotel. It was there. George? George? Where are you? Stop playing silly buggers, George. The hotel's gone waltzing, George. George? Stop it, George. The hotel's gone waltzing, George!

MANDY (*entering with* GEORGETTE): Mum? Mum! There you are! Where the hell have you been? What do you think you're playing at?

ALICE: It's gone waltzing. The hotel. It's not there. George, it's gone waltzing, it's not there.

MANDY: Mum! What are you talking about, Mum? We've been looking everywhere! You can't just go walking off on your own!

GEORGETTE: Don't shout at her, Mandy.

MANDY: Don't tell me what to do!

ALICE: Mandy, your dad... The hotel, it's...

MANDY: It's what, Mum?

ALICE: It's... Erm... It's... I don't know.

MANDY: Of course you don't know!

ALICE: I can't remember.

GEORGETTE: It's all right, love. Calm down.

MANDY: We've been worried sick!

ALICE: Your dad. He's... He's... George? George!

MANDY: Mum, stop it.

ALICE: He's playing silly buggers. He was just here.

MANDY: Mum, will you stop it!

GEORGETTE: Mandy, don't shout at her – remember what I said about patience.

MANDY: Yes, it's all very well you talking about patience, but you don't have to put up with this every day.

GEORGETTE: No, not now I don't, but I did.

MANDY: Oh, and you were always patient, I suppose!

GEORGETTE: Not always, no.

ALICE: George!

MANDY: So what gives you the right to tell me what to do?

GEORGETTE: Nothing, Mandy – I'm just trying to help.

ALICE: Mandy, George!

MANDY: Dad's gone, Mum!

ALICE: Where's he gone? Playing silly buggers.

MANDY: He's not playing silly buggers. Mum, will you at least try and remember?

GEORGETTE: Mandy, don't lose your temper!

MANDY: Stop telling me what to do! Are you so perfect that you never lost your temper?

GEORGETTE: I never said I was perfect. But I know what this kind of anger can lead to, and I don't want to see you make the same mistake I made.

ALICE: George!

MANDY: He died, Mum, remember? Dad – George – is dead.

ALICE: What?

MANDY: He's gone, in the ground.

ALICE: Don't be silly! I was just talking to him.

MANDY: No, Mum, he died, two months ago.

ALICE: Two months…

MANDY: Two months ago. Remember?

ALICE (*pause*): Heart attack? He had a heart attack.

MANDY: That's right.

ALICE: Yes. He was supposed to take me dancing.

MANDY: No, Mum, we were supposed to be going dancing.

ALICE: Yes. We're going to Blackpool.

MANDY: We're in Blackpool, Mum. Look around you. Blackpool!

ALICE: That was quick!

GEORGETTE: Come on. Let's get you back to the hotel.

ALICE: Yes. Are we going dancing?

MANDY: No, Mum. We're not going dancing. The ballroom is closed. Finished. Like this holiday.

ALICE: Closed?

MANDY: Let's get back to the hotel, pack our things and go.

ALICE: Are we not going dancing, then?

MANDY: No.

GEORGETTE: Yes.

MANDY: What?

GEORGETTE (*to* MANDY): I've got an idea.

ALICE: Is it not closed?

GEORGETTE: It's just been moved.

MANDY: Moved?

GEORGETTE (*to* MANDY): Go with me on this.

ALICE: Why did they move it?

GEORGETTE: Refurbishment.

ALICE: I see.

GEORGETTE: Let's get you back to the hotel and cleaned up.

MANDY (*quietly, to* GEORGETTE): What are you doing?

GEORGETTE: I'm helping. At least allow me to do that.

MANDY: I suppose things can't get worse.

SCENE 2

Back at the hotel. GEORGETTE *is just putting up one last string of fairy lights.* MANDY *enters.*

MANDY: Oh Georgette, it looks amazing!

GEORGETTE: Thanks – it's just old curtains, bed sheets and Christmas lights, but it makes it look a little different to usual.

MANDY: It's great. She'll love it. Did you do it all on your own?

GEORGETTE: Well, Tom helped a bit.

MANDY: It's beautiful. Thanks for doing this.

GEORGETTE: It's my pleasure. Thank you for letting me.

MANDY: Don't be silly!

GEORGETTE: I'm glad I've been able to help out.

MANDY: I really appreciate it.

GEORGETTE: I feel like I'm finally doing the right thing.

MANDY: Yes. Thank you. Shall I go and get my mum?

GEORGETTE: Mandy?

MANDY: Yeah?

GEORGETTE: Have you ever… (*Trails off.*)

(*Pause.*)

MANDY: Have I ever what?

GEORGETTE: Have you ever done anything that you regret?

MANDY: What do you mean?

GEORGETTE: Oh, it's nothing.

MANDY: No, go on.

GEORGETTE: If you'd done something you regretted, something you thought was wrong, do you think you'd be able to forgive yourself?

MANDY: Well, I'm not sure. I don't really know what you mean.

GEORGETTE: If you'd done something that you know other people would judge you for.

MANDY: Like what?

GEORGETTE: Well, with my mum things didn't quite go as smoothly as they could've…

MANDY: What do you mean, 'didn't quite go smoothly'?

GEORGETTE: I was struggling to cope.

MANDY: Well, it's difficult. I'm beginning to see that myself.

GEORGETTE: Yes, but I… I didn't deal with everything as well as I could have.

MANDY: I'm sure you did everything you could.

GEORGETTE: No, I didn't.

MANDY: Georgette, are you all right?

GEORGETTE: I can't forgive myself.

MANDY: Georgette?

GEORGETTE: I was at my wits' end, Mandy.

MANDY: It's OK.

GEORGETTE: I was getting so frustrated with her.

MANDY: Of course, I understand.

GEORGETTE: No. No, you don't. You couldn't.

MANDY: Of course I do.

GEORGETTE: No. You don't. One night, after she'd wet herself for the second time in as many hours, I just lost it. I was changing the sheets and I had the pillow in my hand...

MANDY: Georgette?

GEORGETTE: I had the pillow in my hand and... it just seemed like the best thing to do...

MANDY: Georgette, are you saying you...?

GEORGETTE: No. No, I couldn't. But for a second...

MANDY: Thank God.

GEORGETTE: For a second I thought I would. All I had to do was push it down over her face... end it all, for all of us.

MANDY: Yes, but you didn't!

GEORGETTE: No, I didn't, but that was it for me then.

MANDY: What do you mean?

GEORGETTE: I couldn't trust myself, so I left them. I ran away. Left my sister to deal with it on her own.

(*Pause.* MANDY *is speechless.*)

I couldn't cope. I couldn't deal with seeing my own mum disappearing, becoming just a shadow of her former self.

(*Pause.* MANDY *is still gob-smacked.*)

I abandoned them both when they needed me.

(*Pause.* MANDY *is still lost for words.*)

GEORGETTE: I've never forgiven myself.

MANDY: I don't... (*Trails off before she can finish, '...know what to say'.*)

GEORGETTE: I didn't see my mum again after that. I saw my sister at the funeral. She didn't speak.

(*There is a lengthy pause.*)

MANDY: I see.

GEORGETTE: Every day since I've woken up hoping it was all a bad dream, but I have to live with it – I have to live with what I did. And doing this for you lets me feel like I'm giving a little bit back. That perhaps I can forgive myself a little bit. Work off what I did.

MANDY: I don't really know what to say.

GEORGETTE: Don't say anything. I'm just glad I've finally been able to tell somebody what happened. Get it off my chest. Let somebody know that I'm not proud of what I did.

MANDY: No... well...

GEORGETTE: Now, you go and fetch your mum down, and let's have a great night.

MANDY: Sure.

GEORGETTE: I hope you don't feel any differently about me.

MANDY: I've only known you a couple of days – I'm still forming an opinion.

GEORGETTE: Well, I hope you know that deep down I never meant any harm. Maybe you can empathise a little bit?

MANDY: Well. Maybe... I'll go and get my mum.

GEORGETTE: Sure. Mandy? Thanks.

(MANDY *leaves to get* ALICE. GEORGETTE *moves through to the back room and starts the music playing. She returns with a bottle of wine and is filling two glasses as* MANDY *and* ALICE *enter.* ALICE *is wearing a modest ballgown and her dance shoes.*)

MANDY: Here we are, Mum. Come in.
ALICE: Oh yes. Yes. Oh, it's beautiful.
GEORGETTE: Would you like a glass of wine?
ALICE: Yes, please. I... oh, I've forgotten my purse! Mandy I haven't got my purse.
GEORGETTE: That's fine – it's on the house.
ALICE: Are you sure?
GEORGETTE: Positive.
ALICE: Oh, how kind. Thank you. Mandy, wasn't that kind.
MANDY: It was very kind, yes.
GEORGETTE: The pleasure is all mine. Now, please feel free to take a seat, and if you feel like a dance the floor is yours!

(ALICE *and* MANDY *sit down.* GEORGETTE *leaves.*)

ALICE: Isn't it lovely, Mandy!
MANDY: It is.
ALICE: It's certainly different.
MANDY: Yes, you could say that.
ALICE: Thank you for bringing me, Mandy. I know I was stubborn about it, but I'm so glad we came.
MANDY: You're welcome, Mum.
ALICE: And I know it's not easy living with me these days...
MANDY: Mum, you don't need to...
ALICE: But I do appreciate everything you're doing for me.
MANDY: You don't need to thank me, Mum.

ALICE: No, I do. You're taking a lot of time out of your own life to look after me, and although I'm a bit grouchy and stubborn, I want you to know that I'm glad you're there.
MANDY: Thanks, Mum.

(*The music changes to a waltz.*)

ALICE: I got a bit confused earlier when I was on my own. Blackpool isn't how I remember it. I knew where I wanted to go, but nothing looked the same – nothing was right.
MANDY: I know, Mum.

(*They are silent for a moment, and after a second* ALICE *begins to hum along to the waltz.*)

You like this one, don't you?
ALICE: It's my favourite.
MANDY: I thought I recognised it. Would you like to dance?
ALICE: Well, I'll need my dance shoes.
MANDY: You're wearing them, Mum!
ALICE: Oh. So I am. Silly me. I'd love to dance. Thank you.

(*They stand and begin to dance. The music grows.*)

One, two, three. One, two, three.
MANDY (*joining in*): One, two, three. One, two, three.
ALICE: That's it – you're getting it!
MANDY: I have waltzed before, Mum.
ALICE: Could have fooled me. Keep moving.
MANDY: I'm moving, I'm moving!

ALICE: That's it. One, two, three.
MANDY: You've still got it, you know.
ALICE: You never forget. It's like riding a bike.

(*They continue to waltz.*)

When we get back, if you think it's the best thing to do, maybe we should go and see somebody – a doctor – about my memory.
MANDY: Are you sure?
ALICE: Yes. If you think that's best.
MANDY: I do.
ALICE: Yes. Me too.

(*They continue to dance.* ALICE *drifts off into her own world. The song comes to an end.*)

MANDY: I do love you, you know.
ALICE: I know. I love you too, George.

(*The lights fade.*)